Eluding Sylvia, Chasing Poe

A choose-your-own adventure of
Bipolar-Disordered-mood people

Sher'ee Furtak-Ellis

Copyright © 2020 by Sher'ee Furtak-Ellis

All rights
reserved. No part of this
publication may be reproduced,
distributed, or transmitted in any form or by
any means, including photocopying, recording, or
other electronic or mechanical methods, without the
prior written permission of the publisher, except in the
case of brief quotations embodied in critical reviews
and certain other noncommercial uses permitted by
copyright law.

 A catalogue record for this book is available from the National Library of Australia

Sher'ee Furtak-Ellis (author)

ISBN 978-1-922452-09-2
POETRY
MENTAL HEALTH

Typeset Font 11/16

Cover artwork based on original
artwork by Sher'ee Furtak-Ellis
Cover and book design by Green Hill Publishing

Acknowledgements

This is for you, for all of you battling mental illnesses. This is for Sher'ee, without her mind we would not exist. This is for all the experiences she endured, enjoyed, feared, survived, played, used, gained, felt and loved.

Sincerely,

Indira, Jacob, Katherine, Lucy and Stefan (the mood people).

Help and support

Parts of this book may disturb you and trigger unwelcome thoughts. It is not my intention at all, I want this book to uplift and inspire people with mental illnesses. I know first-hand what it is like to have Bipolar Disorder, depression, anxiety, psychosis and panic disorder. I live with it, I write about it, I talk about it. We do not have to feel ashamed anymore, as we know now that we all are affected by mental illness in some way.

Did you know that almost half of all Australians will experience a mental illness at some point in their lifetime? i.e. Anxiety, bipolar disorder, depression, schizophrenia, substance use disorders.

If you feel unwell, mentally or physically, please talk to your GP or mental health professional as soon as you can.

Here are some helpful support lines:

Beyond Blue	1300 22 4636
Headspace - National Youth Mental Health Foundation	1800 063 267
Lifeline	13 11 14
MensLine Australia	1300 78 99 78
Open Arms - Veterans & Families Counselling	1800 011 046
Suicide Call Back Service	1300 659 467

START HERE

SOS

did you hear me?
SOS
Now did you hear me?
I'm in peril
I need help
Please
Someone
Give me something
I don't care
Just put me
Out of my misery
And yours too
SOS
Keep pumping my brain
I am insane
Please
Doctor
Which one are you now?
Just give me sanity, security and nourishment
I'll give you me
And my life stories
For your entertainment
And
Experience.

WHICH BIPOLAR MOOD CHOOSES YOU TODAY?

Adventurous – go to page 85
Peaceful – go to page 39
Melancholy – go to page 67
Loving – go to page 50
Spiritual – go to page 3
Euphoria – go to page 18

INDIRA

LOVERS' GARDEN

See the maroon curtains hang over his windows gloomily
His eyes like a black lace veil on a mourner at a funeral
Of someone they loved dearly and lusted occasionally

With blackened tears and a hardened heart,
She cries to tunes of death
And perishes prettily

He says "in my angry slumber I feel so serene
And nightmares travel swiftly
Like flying knives slicing at every crevice and
I love it"

I have been wrong and so have you
But this lovers according to moods fiasco
Is ruining my tranquil garden, like a plague

Ending a love that came to us, we're saying our farewells
The damned boy slides onto a boat and drifts away upon a
    sea so salty
Wondering if I'd love you again one day
NO WAY!
Brown eyes always run and stain
My green eyes will regain
Singing songs of pain
And the tragic, idealistic, yearning lady
Will cry so hard, so very, very hard
And get stray
And feral
And yet she will survive
So Goodbye!

APATHY AND JAZZ

filthy ludicrousness
cringing, overhanging
lingering on
odium score
mystical second glance
poseur, existing a pristine creature
closet matron, majestic sinner
time shoots exquisitely, unaffected
dementia partner, concerning love
unable to see, nowhere present
shake my creed, head weak
devour the species, greedy little thing
lost subconscious, vixen existin'
apart/condensed, parallel friend
rhythm smooth, silken sounds
drastic jokes, excessive paint
lifting walls, barrier broken…
and now you can get to know me

CHEATED

past the felt sensational hole
clear hand dealt to a suffragette
changing the cards to master a technique
washing the path and cleansing the dream
changing the past and mastering a scheme
playing the deal with an ace in the team
you're giving me the urge to kill what hurts
mixing perception and comprehension
Did I hear that right?
Idiot pursuit, a foolish game to play
She loves to manipulate the wrong doers
And justify her loss
To earn a win
And retain a poker grin

DREAMS ASIDE

"Although the dream subsides
you'll satisfy the ride", she says rationally as
the calm disgusts and runs away
I deceived myself as I watched the star glimmer and glow profusely
But how is that?
Respect denied and trouble lies
dormant
While loneliness grows
The problems still exist
And I know they must be sorted
To get my life in order
But cheating the morals I once had
Will not achieve the dream
Cut me deeper, your knife is larger
My weapon is only my tongue
But her voice is no good today
So have me, consume me, need me temporarily
For I am the only piece in your puzzle
That does not fit.
I want to have the last laugh
Because I know
your success remains beer and nuts
Whilst mine will be champagne.
So eat your thoughts,
your dirty lying words
And keep my face inside
Because
I won't forget you.
My blade pursues
I am coming for you

WINDSCREENS

Back in the glass case
Dreaming of old days
Flying around my town
Lost in my new ways

Crying hearts run
Out of this body
Out of this mind
But I'll still love you
And all the silly things you do

Leap into the road you've been wanting to take
Drive down the highway
With dust in your eyes
And showers on your mind
Loving it and singing with the birds in the sky
Staring out the front and
Up into the blue
Dirt on the windscreen
where's the Windex?

FESTIVE DINING

Pebbles scattered on silky sand
Not man-made
Arrived there themselves
With cockles
Warm cans of soft drink
Hard to swallow
Sweetness fading
Turns to mellow
Hard seeds ripening
Green to red
Tan to tangerine
Softening
Ready for harvesting
Bite and eat
Drink in Crete
Delicious and sweet
Fruitful muse
Wafts of enchanting aromas
From simple stoves
Complex recipes
Labours of love
A dash of hope
Lashings of flavour
Conclusion tasty collusion
Effort rewarded
With smiles, burps and clean plates.

SLEEPING LETS ME DIE FOR A SHORT WHILE

Sleeping allows my brain to reset
Sleeping gives me time to breathe deeply
Sleeping pauses the chaos in my mind
Sleeping refreshes my irregular heartbeat
Sleeping provides numbing for my cramped feet
Sleeping heals the opened wounds closed
Sleeping avoids when gusty winds blow
Sleeping stops me from weeping
Sleeping is kindness to my tired body
Sleeping cleanses my stinging eyes
Sleeping lets me escape to other worlds
But
Sleeping when you are on trial could be the death of you…

THE FUNERAL

We stand beside
Pallor mortis here
Numb from hurt
Cold and fearful
The world is vengeful
So to the light we are beckoned
Release the pain
Abandon our old ways
Bid your farewells
To people you may not know
Then action your plans
Ideas of paradise
Emancipating
Today

ALLIGATOR GORGE, MOUNT REMARKABLE

We trek through ancient rock walls
Still smelling the bones of extinct crustaceans
A rainbow colours our path as
We delve deeper into the past
I lose my shoe in the knee-deep water and panic as
I envision alligators scooping it up and swallowing whole
I jump onto my father's back looking down curiously
We continue towards the sky, climbing over colonies of baby
    mammals
A miniature world inside a gigantic gorge
Photographs cannot even reveal the true beauty of this place
For progress did not touch this land, time stood stubbornly
Proud

ANGRY WITH MYSELF FOR FALLING VICTIM (TEMPORARILY) TO AN EMOTIONAL VAMPIRE

Heart pounding
Air inhaled frantically
Steaming, fuming, wishing cruelty upon you
I think you are a faker, riding on coat tails, flying upon blackened wings
You'll get what you deserve
When the time is right
When the moon is clear and the air is still
The coldness in your heart and the pretence in your eyes giving me the chills
Your soul had died, reborn to ash
Bereft of honest visions
Closeness becomes vacuous
You will crumble when the world realises
the evil behind your kindness
Same old commissionaire stare enchanting people with gleaming eyes
Seers will recede, for we know the truth
Nothing but emptiness.

俳句

1.
The first autopsy
Done in silence
Albeit the drips, cuts and groans

2.
He told me he hated mathematics
However
He loved computers

3.
Wondrous pleasure
She sighs
And reciprocates

4.
Human longevity
Discoveries
We always thought it was a gas

SCARS

Wearing paternal scars
Inside my chest
Like a block of
Hardened cheese
Clogging my veins
Awaiting the next hit
We cried, tears of relief now
That we're no longer those
Angry children, confused about how to
Aim
How to swear on our own two feet that
Life was viewed from dark glasses upturned in séances
Unleashing demons, housebound angels once houseproud now
Burning kitchens down to the ground
Spaghetti stains the kitchen ceiling
Broken glass shards impale the linoleum
Violent sprays echo through the hallway
Bruising fades, bones heal sideways
Blood clots remain
And wounds are still open
Until
They congeal and heal

THE JOURNEY

"Is she here?" the girl kept asking, as the water slid along the dream-pipes. She shivers as she waits because she knows she's done the wrong thing, again. She's on some tripped-out planet. Her hair flows like the breeze. Her brain is fuzzy like fairy floss and I'm not supposed to understand… how the rain falls on her precious, loopy head and only sweat gathers on mine. She says that "God rains on those who are high enough to receive" but I am so low, I cannot know.

But wait, there's a lush green patch over the rainbow and I'm heading for it.

ARE YOU GOING TO:

Go slow? Go to page 3
Pace and spy like a predator? Go to Page 39
Run like hell? Go to page 18
Indulge in every vice? Go to page 85
Make sweet love? Go to page 50
Think about it? Go to page 67

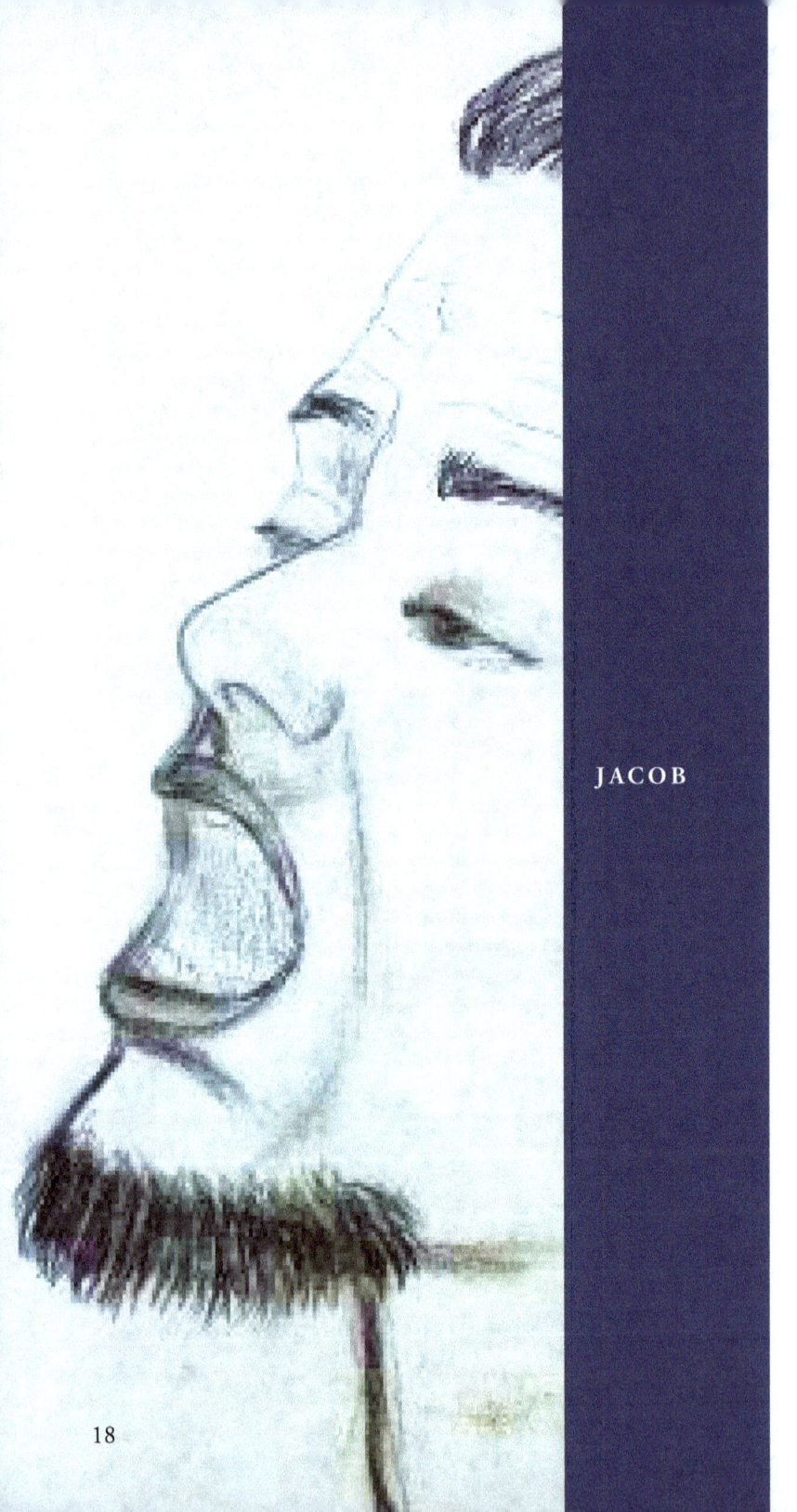

JACOB

NURSE LUCY.

she's just like an angel to me
her white bits show where the brown once sat freely
she seems so delicate
but you'll get to know her strength
underneath the impish façade
lazy days, playing in the sunshine
with cats and dogs and birds and wolves
it feels so good
it is good
if you find her flakey
go see the fun
she's not letting on
her mind expands to where others fear to tread

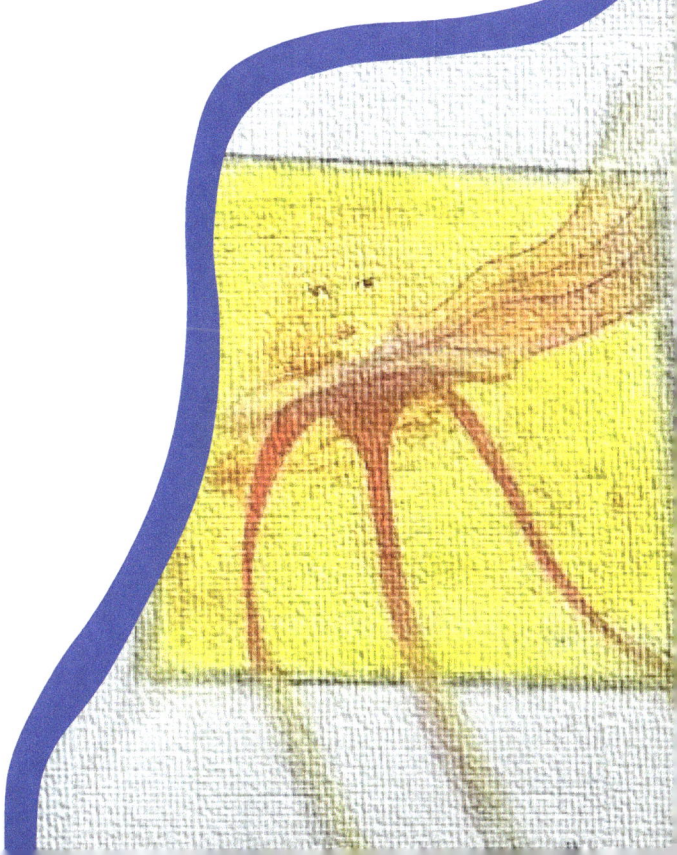

HELD

Faced the sun
Got burnt and blistered
Moved to the Arctic
Got frozen and frost-bitten
Walked in the desert
Got dehydrated and desecrated
Lazed in the tropics
Got dense and diabetic
Worked in a temperature-controlled office and
Woke up brain-dead.

INSUBORDINATE

Learn the rules
Ways and styles
Of us

Buy the clothes
Walk the talk
Age gracefully
Like us

Forget your past
Clear today
Act natural
Join us

Sustain insane
Wealth and power
Argue
With us

You will succeed, just as long as you do it – with US!

MUSIC

Great sounds, but it's not music
Unless there's a story
And the right voice to tell it
A person with experience
Can scream and cry
Unlike the noob who
Whines and groans
Words with no meaning
Ahead of an orchestra
Performing tunes
The audience becomes
Immune
So one must evolve
And divulge
All their naughty little secrets into
A composition of
Amazement

HURTING KIND

Crushed egos, broken will
his heart is heavy and no pill could
fix him
if the winds lift him up today, he cries "i swear
i could fly away, forever"
opening his vision to the greatness of nature
deserted on a platelet
hesitating
impatiently waiting for the tornado to
snatch him
and curse him
curling tumbleweeds roll down the
abandoned road, chasing ghosts
he chased your dream
not asking for the responsibility
not reeping what you have sown
no faith in love or
loyalty to a memory
a memory
floats
into aeons
losing itself
ending an ideal once shared
begone child, you are far gone!
melting off the snow fields
you went, you ran and
dove for the notion of
fantastique

but you failed to find it
u disappeared
u fell out of
photographs
images collected through a time of passion
u took off
crossing highways, dodging cars
you saw her
with silky hair flowing
gently breezing
in the dirt
she falls hard and
forgets, picks up her bones
brushes herself off with
scraped and bleeding hands
up and on to go running
why?
because she has cravings
for adventure
and mayhem
so much to see in Syria and Libya
she dreams of the chaos of her youth
touching freedom
watching violence
hearing torture
murdered
scenes she's seen before but
no resolve
nightmares
idling away in the corners of her mind
seriously cracking her heart
breaking cherubs

urge to call her posse
escape to nowhere, with no-one
wrangle up a ghost-crew
kick up the dust
booting boulders under the sun
warming
she runs
a warning
skin burning
innards cooking
dehydrate, digest, beg
plead
for mercy
going blank and yet content with
nothing she needs but
everything she wants
weird
are you muted, or, mutable?
jaded or crystallised?
make up your split-mind!
Are you worth his devotion?
One could wonder…

8 PLANES DOWN

Catastrophe seen from our table
Upon the hill
A cocktail resting
Our heads full tilt upward
Watching the jets and rockets
UP – CURVE – DOWN
Crashing into ceremonial land
Time is spared for us
We read the logos – Rex, Qantas, Virgin, Singapore, Cathay, Malaysia, Emirates
Our hearts skip a beat as the disaster unfolds
We run from the bar and into the botanical gardens
Memories of city shops and familiar stops now warped into oblivion
Running, running, confused we run
Gathering friends, citizens, servants of the government
Out to the park lands, across the broken roads, towards the beach
Clustering, conjuring, covering under the robust red bones of an old railway bridge
Beams held together by massive engineered bolts and rivets
West of the catastrophe, circling 5, within the land we wait hoping that
Mad Max arrives in a junk-trap vehicle able to withstand the explosions, the heat, the gases, the dead-fumes and bloody water
We wait
Underneath the beams
In hope we can start again in
The end of tyranny and
The beginning of victory.

Drink some more liquid courage
Deceiver
Continue taking those ales
Deceiver
Keep smoking your serum
Deceiver
Compliment your public
Deceiver
Join in on the parodies
Deceiver
Declare your motions proud
Deceiver
Bow your head to the demons below
Deceiver
Attack the lovers
Deceiver
You cannot control what you fail to know
Deceiver
Unleashed darkness within
Deceiver you must
Leave.

HAZY

Death is pain
Pain is death
I'll drink my blood of death
& die in pain
for this fulfils me
more than life
the ultimate death
the blood I tasted
for a long time
was so bitter but
now it refreshes and calms my restless soul
to the point that my soul becomes rested
so I then realise that there is no god, there is no heaven,
there is only us and our twisted mind that kills me
and You who tries to kill me with pills… but sadly I'm already
　　dead

I don't understand what my mind is trying to tell me
I've been through it this time and now my thoughts are coming
　　clearly
I contemplate a way for living in this hell
and pushing your thought pellets won't make a way for me to tell
Coz my eyes are going hazy
And they say it's just a phase I'm going through

I don't feel good – painful face
I exaggerate my simplicity – because I'm scared of the human race
I want the thoughts to stop – so I can find out what's on the other
　　side
I have appeared so normal for such a long time now – but isn't it
　　time to face the truth
I have a manic twin… he's a big bad boy with a lust for life, ready
　　to party, ready for strife!

And the other twin… he's boring, brainy and burning with ambition!
But does he know what others think?
Does he care what they think?
Keeping people happy, what a chore, what a past-time?!?
Stable isn't normal anyhow.

EXHAUSTION

My body is tired but I can't sleep
There's too much to think about
I'm biting my thin skin and listening in
To everything they say above and
The laughter is aimed at me I swear

I am me, but I'm afraid I'll always be me
And it scares me man!
[Screams]
Let me out

But here right now, I stand tall and proud
Of all the achievements I made
So what if it's not about me,
or the way I have ever been?

EPISODE NO. 348728739 ELTHAM VIC

A mess of smudged mascara
Twisted, hurting and in pain
Emotionally unstable for an hour or two
You plod onwards to your dreams
You are alone but not insane
Your muddled thoughts might be their gain
Let your tears stain and refrain from your facials
Compose yourself, cover your soul with grace and
Learn to carry on even though
It is hard to see when
the kaleidoscope of colours are clouding your vision
Rainbows beckon but
How do you get there?
You must collect the maps and timetables and
Hope for all your worst nightmares to go away
Although your masochistic-hotel-room rage won't
Let you see beyond the grimy, bloody gnomes hacking at you with
Imaginary garden tools and smashing handfuls of
Fresh cow manure at your face
Oh what a disgrace!

THE 241

splash around the tainted window
wild water of joy and prosperity
glazy, hazy at times
clustering into profound faith
or to what seems right for you
and bad just doesn't enter
no grim thoughts enter your mind
of flames between silk
eating my heart out with your deception
gusts of leaves and wilting trees
tell me you will come over
I won't need to ask
I will be prepared
All this from one whose importance burdens its own face
The air that fills your mattress won't be mine
Definitely another saints'
Another angel alights

LOVE IS LOVE

I love
You love
The difference is
I do not want to be known for only
My sexuality
My sex life is private
As is yours
I seal my commitment as
Do yours
But yours is accepted as
Real yet
Mine is denounced as
Frivolous
Unnecessary and
Unjust
Trivial.

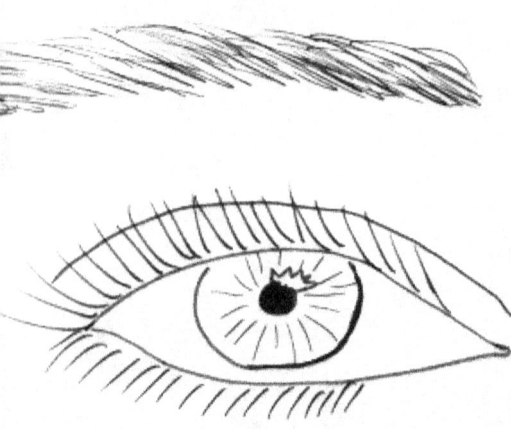

COBRA

A bulky vineyard covers cracked soil
Cobra slides away
Wineglass slips from jittery hand
Shatters into concrete ground
Slivers are sharp, beware
Cobra disorientated splits its skin
Breaking, bleeding
United bloody hands touch injured cloak
The cobra wails and hisses, unable to respond like it should
Life expiring, awkward fingers scoop the mush of entrails, broken
    scales as
Head and beady eyes tire, subdued, blackout
In and out, a white cloth bag
Cobra trapped, engine fires, motoring
Uncovered, unwrapped, the rangers eyes meet the
Cobra's, they've met before but this time
Human controls reptile

INDIFFERENT

State of mind, what we deal, what we feel
He says "Smile for the hurt ones,
Hug the earth,
Peace out to all"
Beauty in your thoughts and words
I hear right through to my bones
Elevates my muscles, my spine rises
Perfect calm in a perfect storm
It is our decade for chaos and burden
Yearning for that comfortable, country life
Vivid colours dance
Rivers, streams, floating me further down, down, down
Are you ready babe?
Watch the clock tower
Wondering if we're all going to be punctual for once in our lives!
You know, just cruisin', chillin'
so what if
the god of Mars liked lots of arse and
the goddess of Venus liked lots of penis?
Is it really anyone's business?
Hey there nonchalant kid:
Wake
The
Fuck
Up!

LIMBO

There's beauty in the darkness
A light bit of comfortable
Elephants dancing in the wind
And a dry storm is coming to
Blow away all your fears
Cold is not a good pain
And emptiness sucks too much so
You won't see inside minds eyes
For life is so good and appealing that it's
Covering up all your tears
In a warm, shaded and calm veneer
The words you say are very fair
And clear.
Clear enough to,
To make things all confused
"Get whatever you see and
Earn the life you want" is all I ever hear.
Why am I so indecisive?

"PREPARE FOR DOOM!"

he warns of chaos in both the inner and outer world.
"Don't waste a moment! Gather your armour!"
he comes to read the Good News to me but I'm a Gemini-rising,
   I like to tell the tales. A modern spiritualist confused by the
   overload of 'truth's', punished by verses with no version-con-
   trol. Behold the supreme ruler is watching your every move
   while sunshine-flavoured poultry is devoured nightly, with
   roasted crackling of unclean swine.
Cold war is over, hot battles begin to rage…

WHERE WILL YOU GO TO?

Battle? Go to page 85
Hills? Go to Page 39
Safety? Go to page 67
Surrender? Go to page 18
Mediation? Go to page 50
Pray? Go to page 3

KATHERINE

KOALA

I am a koala
Resting in trees
Munching on leaves
Eucalyptus dreaming
Warm winds
Branches holding me
Only enough teeth for uses simple
My needs are few and far between
Soft fur, easily hurt
Great for calm cuddles
I am a koala
Serene

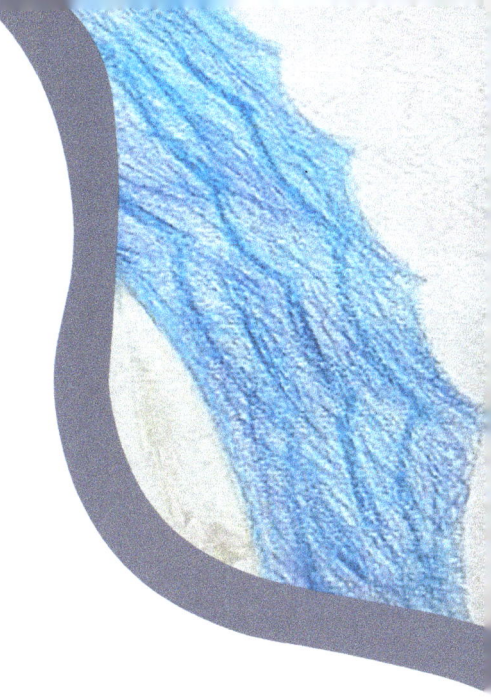

MARINER

A parachute marina
Brightest blue water
A boat rests calmly
Bathing beauties smiling
A white wall surrounds us
Soft sunshine warming
A fence of yellow tape
Safely waking me
A scream heard earlier
Blanketed out
A fun-filled day to be had
Basking in pleasance upon
The sparkling ocean ebbing and flowing
Bells ring loudly, proudly
Tea upon the deck
While the world keeps turning

HEALING SISTERS
(FOR KYLIE AND TANYA)

She bathes
Unclothed, unbetrothed
Steam rises from still water in a
Pool filled with nymphs and
Soul sisters
Calm
Unadorned
Mermaidens gather with
Messages clear and
She floats into
Soothing bath
They grieve together
For an unknown child
Healing slowly in
Memorium

She sees through
Moist air in a majestic hall
Deservedly
Cleansed
By stream, by waterfall
The four maids fair, soft
Dreaming

BITTERSWEET

It is bittersweet, rejoicing
A triumph in art
Appreciating
Human beauty
While
A friend, a living being
Says goodbye
Slipping away into the sky
Atoms to atoms
Cosmic dust.
I will remember
Your goodness
Your security
Your sadness.
Let them forgive
It was not intentional
Only circumstance
Surrounds
The actions
Of a tormented soul.
Let him go
Let his soul be free
Let go of bitter thoughts
And sour feelings
Don't wallow in self-pity
Or you'll be haunted
Resentful
Hurt
By his words
and his wounds, so
Close them
With strong, bonding sutures
Healing families
Lost loves
Time to cherish
Honest memoirs of
Joyful times together, and
   remember the…
serenity.

GOLDMINING

Loyal to a panning-man
She sifts in and out of his heart
Then glass rooftops smash and
Precarious tree tops surrender
Birds make blunders
Jumping into the burning pot
Her poor hands, her worth is
Washed away with gold-tailings
Dazed and wasted
She remains at his side
Flicking the dust off his strides
His left hand
Her right hip
Firmly planted

ALONE

Waiting in hollow
She breathes in doubt
Exhales finality
And asks herself
Is that it?
She thought
She was destined for greater adventures
Pure exploration of the universe
Creating life
And art
That dream was plagiarised
Stolen harmony
Peace destroyed for
Germination of hybrid seeds
Not wholesome unions
As once were believed to be
She inhales brand new air
Complete in isolation
A loner
Incomplete.

FOREVER

you love for real and I love your feel
two lips and one mouth are so close
but drifting further apart from a fairytale
sealing a sweet and seething end
Forever
I love to tempt you into three lives
Whether or not we can work it out
Or slide into obscurity for good
Mending hearts that could be together
Forever
You want to tell me something
But words seem to escape the mind
Why can't you just do it and do it beautifully
To bring about this harmony
We've been waiting a long time
for
Ever

Bicycles and buses
Take me to Yum Cha
Step off the bus and into the smells, sights and tastes of Chinatown
Hot dogs at the old bus depot shop
Back lane divided
Hidden office compounds
New enclosure
The breakwater
between
Rushing waves of exotic flavour and
Quiet thought sands upon corporate shores

BOWEN STREET, ADELAIDE, 2013.

CLIMAX

To be part of a forlorn life
Our sky is always grey
Doing what we do
Flying
Eating
Walking
Drinking
Sleeping
Dreaming
Caressing
Dancing
Screaming
Demonising
Crouching in the corner
Cleaning skirting boards
While your heart endures
A crushing human blow
Yell, smack, snort, groan
Your life is
Dispersed into several dying pieces
Hang on!!
This is not what you envisioned.

WHAT ARE YOU GOING TO DO?

Cry – go to page 50
Lie – go to page 39
Run – go to page 85
Fight – go to page 18
Wallow – go to page 67
Shout – go to page 3

LUCY

ALF REDUX COSMOS DIVIDUS

Alien messiah
Here beside you
An impression of a mammal
On its' humanoid excursion
You've sensed the being is empty
Nothing behind those spheric eyes
A soul-less embrace
From a line-etched face
Is it real or is it fake?
Souls waiting in space
on coat-hangers above the clouds
Universal bells start chiming
Another species has been born
Float off the rack, descend to Earth
A planet full of life
Slowly becoming inhabited with wise ones
Learned.
Centuries of experience and knowledge
Reincarnated and evolving
Creating and improving
Embracing their path of
Amnesia then anxiety
Void
ALF's we are
Spirit black as nigh
Outer is us
Viewed every man
Creature from afar
Bring forth oceans full of tidal waves
Volcanoes spilling molten lava
Meteors striking arid land
Molecules and matter
Space stations in all corners of the galaxy
Universes full and plenty

Juxtapose and separate
Exist as a few little species
Safe to be wondrously kind and robotic
Not to discover
The ALF in me and you

UNI

I'm so sad, so sad to say
Society took my soul away
I took the pill and it took me
Now here I sit gloomily

I've tried to satisfy them all
They want me, but not me whole
So I play the part with a hint of truth
Whilst they be them and I'll be youth

I don't think that I am old
Though I can't recall the stories told
Things I've said with no remorse
I'd scream and yell till my throat was hoarse

And then, you and I sit side by side
But only one enjoys an easy ride
We read and chat and drink coffee
Smoke and quote philosophies

You know, they know, but I won't ever
I was brought up in the land of never
"You won't get far if you don't get out"
the preachers from the front bar shout

I have heard it is a disease
Sometimes you're immune and through it you'll breeze
But people are people so why should it be that
The feeble burn like fire and the tough never see?

LAND OF GENESIS

The sand breaks asunder
As we walk
Towards our horses
And climb upon our stallion
To ride into the sunset
Smothered with jarring heat
Crooked bones, muscles snake
Fur is grey
Talk is bare
Journeying for miles and miles and miles and miles
We reach the palace in the desert
Our sanctuary, our home
Every luxury is offering
There is no need to leave
Nor explore the other side
Here is your paradise
Evil lies in farther down
Often in the southern city
Where they eat blood-red grapes whilst resting on linen
Enjoying life's little delicacies
As warfare over flocks occurs
And cosmic battles rage on
For who is the ultimate God
That reigns above our families

GHOST IN A MACHINE

Happily typing on the keys
My face suddenly flushes
Letters and numbers appear on my page
Frighteningly automatic they write by themselves
"Is my monitor malfunctioning?" I ask myself
The screen fades to black and
The room gets chilly
Icy stillness enwraps me, as the PC begins to glow
I sit still and patiently wait for
The jumbled mass to form as words
It tells me the time (23 minutes ago)
It says hello ("HeLLo!")
It types ("Goodby Babey")

And disappears.
I run from the room to
Find my brother who stands at
The front door talking
To a woman who sounds like my mother talking to a
Man with a CB radio. A cop?
I shriek loudly, it startles my brother who
Is screaming to my mother "but Why? Why?".
As it turns out, our little brother has just passed away
In a road near Mount Lofty TV towers whilst
Riding his motorbike,
That same moment of time (23+3 minutes ago)
when
He spoke from the other-side.
There have been other moments since then
When his spirit matter comes to
Visit, like yesterday in the lounge-room I
Turned on the TV and
A bright blue light turned up instead
Of Oprah!
But then again, he always liked her.

FRUIT

I am a ghost of me
dark and morose, blue and black
I retrace my own footsteps in
The darkness of the hallway
Minds unkind, my brain is tied and bound
Like a bag of oranges waiting
On the supermarket shelf for someone to
Take me by the hand and
Juice and grate my skin and flesh
Until I am nothing but pulped
Translucent orange
Liquid

THE BUSH-GHOST

I remain and I reside
At the house on Marulan Hill
Among the trees and the picket fences
And the dairy cows and cats meeowing
The sunshine, the frost
Chilly autumn nights
And the lost, the living
I stand waiting at the front door
For you to come home,
Make sure you arrive safely
Make sure you take your shoes off
Make sure you wash your hair
Make sure your bed clothes are laid
And your repellent is switched on
We've been through the minds of our babes
And out through the mouths of the wise
Now
Sky and stars

Moon and Mars
Bricks and bars
Trucks and cars
Eerily I stand there at the edge of your bed
Speaking in mute
Performing ordinary duties in an extraordinary life
I wonder what is good about me
Once in a while
No one answers
The soul of my husband is nowhere to be seen
He's run off with the neighbour's daughter
To greener pastures
I float back down to our Paper Moon Town

GIVE TO LIVE

To live
Working
Buying trips
Just to watch my family die
It's not a very interesting life
Boring and predictable
Saddening.
People say if I keep kicking this black dog
They're going to call the RSPCA
Damn
Am I having a great day?
1 hour on a train
2 hours on a plane
3 hours in a car
4 hours in a bar
5 lonely nights
6 broken fights
7 days of madness
8 ways to get there
9 streets are taken
10 naughty children
11 tired adults
12 Coopers Ale
And some time to write poetry.
Why does the world have numbers
And time
And places
And dirty, dirty cities?
Lost my heart in that dirty, dirty city
and then it returned
Something I know I've learned is
Heartbreak can happen
If you don't pay attention
Lurking behind

Just to creep up on you
When you are not ready
To deal with
It

FAIRYTALES

Unfinished stories
Scattered
In tatters
Uncared for
What does it mean?
What is love?
All I see is
Empty houses
Bare floors
Speckled with dust
Only fluff
Silence
Loneliness
Charmed then
Betrayed

3 AM

This is the time
3 am
this time I won't worry
I'll contemplate and wonder
Why her intoxicated bloody smile
Would make me laugh
And the long talks flowed
Her wisdom amazed me
Yet her stupidity astounded me
Love is really blind
God please make lust a virtue
Then she'll be ok
The journeys taken together
What was I to know?
Wasn't I always there?
Elapsed memory I guess
Well, we can't go back now
It's all over
Build a bridge little girl and be
An adult daughter

EASTER ON THE BEACH

Chocolate and sand on an Autumn day
Wading through miniature waves
Rex and co are happily playing
Slightly burning
No worries
Satan's creatures swarming my face
Telling me stories of our disgrace
Sudden loudness of crashing water unto shore
Can't hear your sermons, can only see colours
Like we've seen before
We're living in the future
Not dwelling on ancient sorrow
Remembering the concept, the foundation of a daydream
Time to harvest
Reap the past with heavy metal faith machines
Stampede on crops with pounding boots
Let those who doubt wither away
For they don't believe
But they will eat
Chocolate and wade in sand on an Autumn day
Ensuring their path to Paradise
With glimmers of spiritual thoughts
Thanks-giving
Safe-haven
Filled with images of Caviezel
Lugging props around forged darkness
Acting as saviour
He wins the award and
Rushes home to

Be alone
Your idol also eats
Rabbits and eggs
Although he's not religious, it's
Ingrained in him, the fable and
The folly.

IN A FEW

In a few more days
Those flowers will turn into fruit
And the leaves will wither
Along with the petals

In a few more weeks
I will wish that I had the courage to speak
On the tram that day
To tell you how much I missed you

In a few more months
The fruit will have long been eaten
Her legs will be swimming in a sea of amniotic fluid
Reminding me through kicks that it's just the two of us

In a few more years
Us two will be catching the tram
We will see him
And he will come to know that
Those few moments will last a lifetime

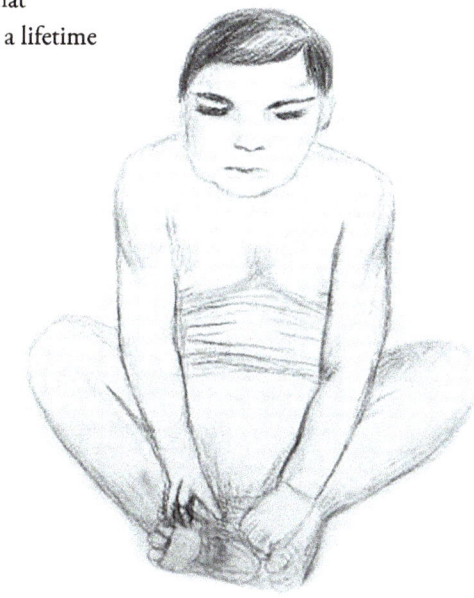

RECOVERY

I am known
For me
Just the girl I've always been
Not an illness or an image
But a person who feels
And I feel happy to be me
Glad to be here in this sanctuary
That is never sold or abused
It is so good
To be loved
For me
I love you all too
And I hope it doesn't fade away
Compassion never really dies
It just gets covered
then uncovered
And rediscovered
Hopefully not exploited
Peace is all we need
Understanding is all we wish for

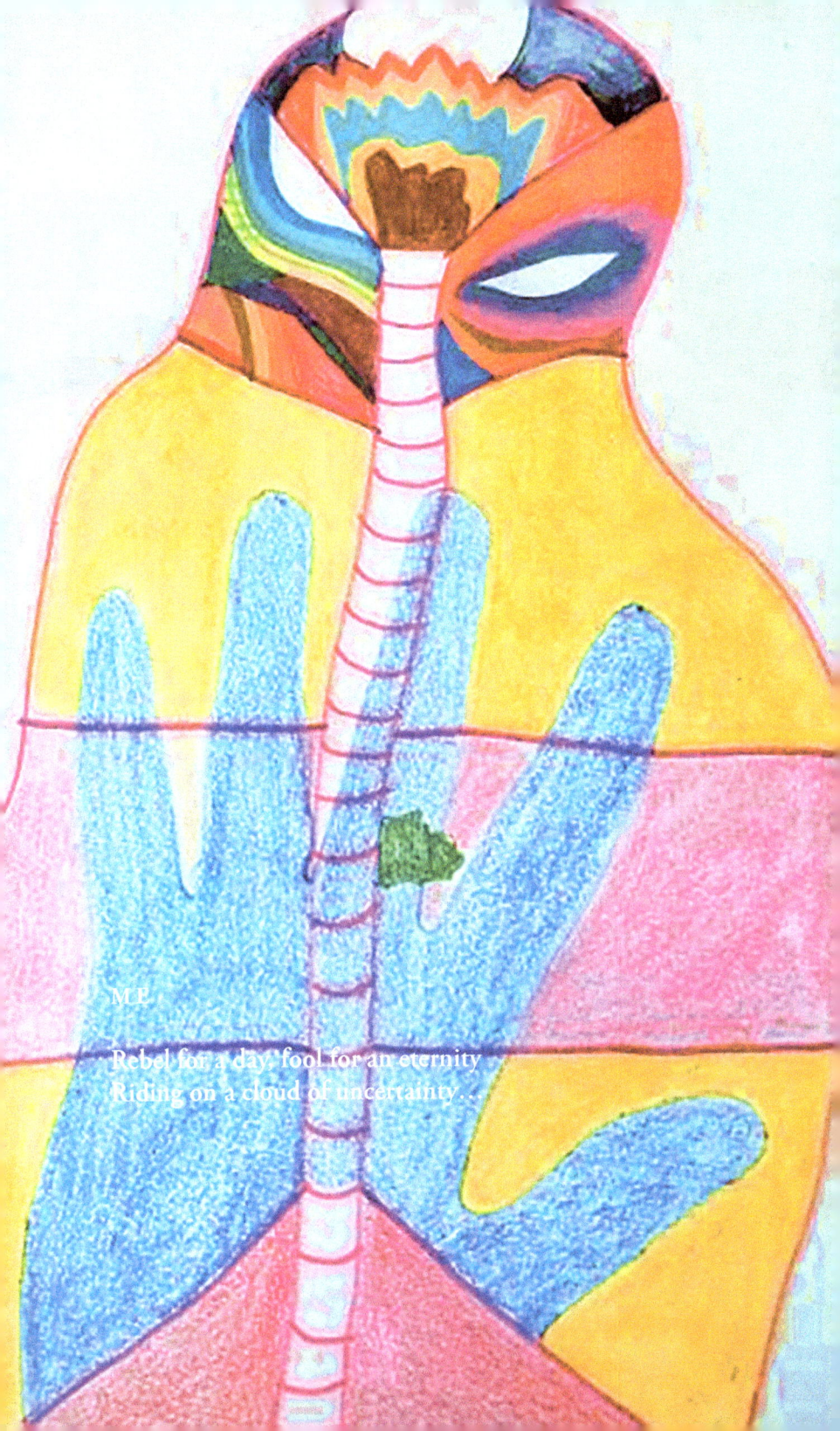

Humidity
Softens my shell
Leaving me vulnerable
Damnum cray
Reborn
Rain washes away
Decades
Of robust wars
My armour
Has been well-worn
Husks adorn
Scars, cuts, dents and craters
Deep in the sea
Not flowing with the tide
Resisting
Centuries
Of hatred and depravity
A perverse reality
Oceans
Oceanides
Across the water
The sun will shine
With warmth from glowing rays
Awakening her dormant spirit
Frozen in the snow
She will emerge
Icebergs shall crush, shatter the rush
Off she goes
New life aquatic calls
Buoyancy, floating me
Holding me steady
Wading through a mystery
An ocean filled with colours, greenery
Sea creatures greeting each
Ebb and flow
Ripples below

Tepid, soft to touch
Stop me from drowning
But let me grow
The journey is just beginning
Down below

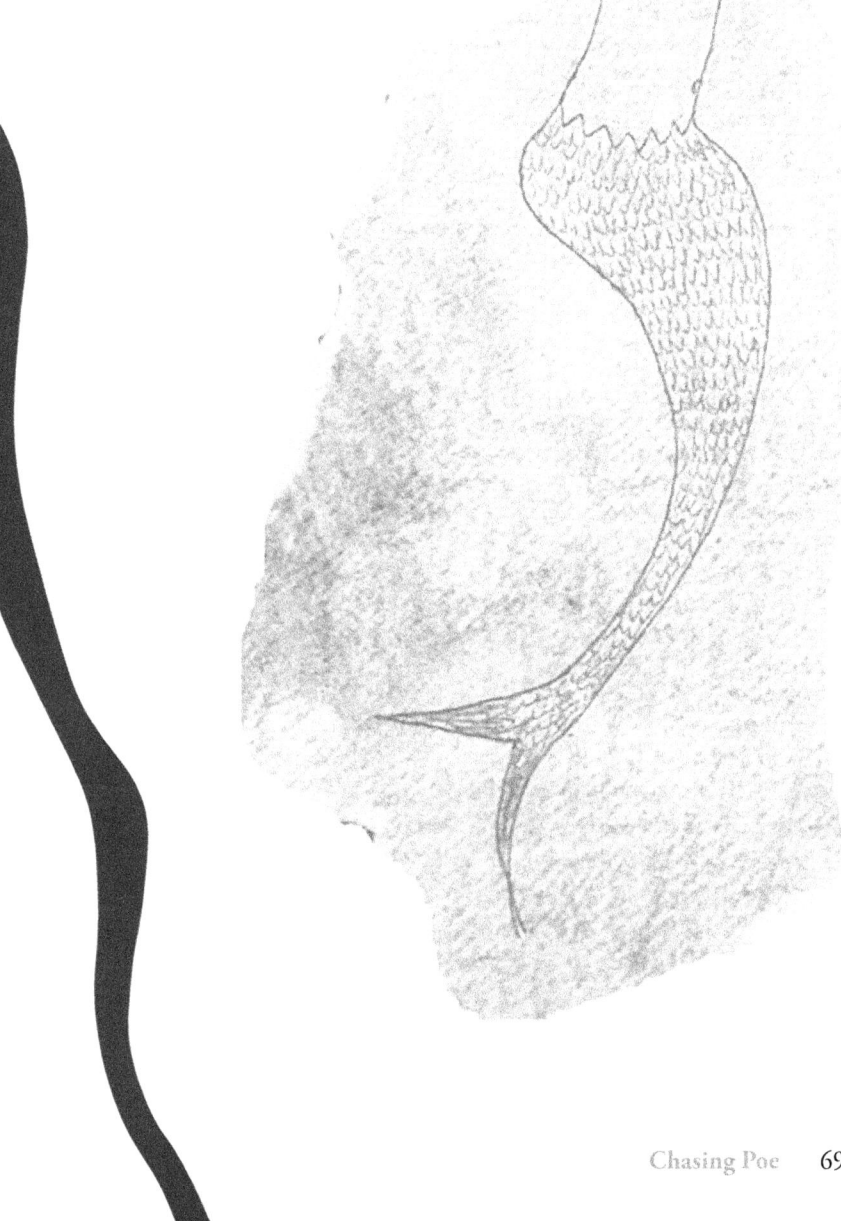

NEW DOOM, OLD TOWN

Standing at the pipeline
Looking in the distance
Darkness getting closer
Shadows in my view
Feel the tension surrounding
Start to kneel below
See the metal shining
Something's going down
Argumentative little fella's
Will slash at each other
And the knife is sharp enough
To disembowel the weaker
His guts drop on the ground
The perpetrator sprints like lightning
The victim plummets forward
His head cracks on the pavement
a mangled mess evident
plasma pools around the cracks in the pavement
I am stunned but run to the phone-box and
call 000 saying 'I do not know how this happened
I was just walking past and stumbled upon a broken man
He ain't got long so come as fast as you can'
The receiver is dropped as I flop
But I've got to go home
Safe in the womb
Even though they're never there
So why am I here?
Because this shelter is my lair
The mad men can still come
Knocking on my windows
Shattering our peace with rumbles of angry thunder
Legs should not tremble
But pink knees always get weak
Hide amid the black and

hope they don't come back
Pray to the one who rules the universe
And wait for morning to break
Or for sirens to wail…
They shall not fail
Safe at last!

PIXIE TERROR

Demolishing more than one apple
once restrained in a fruit-bowl chapel
discomfort in the tidings of
eased and relaxed feet
I get lumps on inky creations
causing maximum distress of course
in an attempt of passaging the planes and putting together all the
    pieces
in a life uncertain of spaceships
rocketing an extraordinary coordination

Daddy is…… a HANDYMAN
                FUNNY MAN
                    SWEET MAN
                      BAR MAN
                        QUIET MAN
                        SENSITIVE MAN
                    SMART MAN
                GIVING MAN
            RESERVED MAN
        WISE MAN
He was my Father.

THE RED DRAGON, THE BLACK DOG & OTHER COLOURFUL CREATURES

My anger, my pain, my fear, my hurt and my hatred is their gain
My anger, my pain, my fear and my hurt is their gain
My anger, my pain and my fear is their gain
My anger and my pain is their gain
My anger is their gain
My pain is my gain

BLUEBIRD
bluebird travels at a hundred miles
you won't be sleeping when the sun will rise
fly high,
soar above the mountains
with an eagle by your side
on a quest to see your flesh and bloods
you arrive to a scene of dread
eyes open wide and mouths shut tight
they're not sleeping, they have died.
Your blue wings turn to grey… fly, fly away

CHANGES DON'T WAIT *(FOR SIMON)*

You've always been so sweet to me
Gentle voice and eyes beyond the ocean's blue
Below desert skies
I see now
Turning my life around
I'm wearing a crown
Thinking hats abound
Let's get this idea down
These green eyes are going crazy!
The illustrations are in your mind
Soul-man still lingers
The black dog still barks
Dragons still wake you
Angel-mates still haunt you
But knives are back in the drawer
Especially when you have finally found
Ways to balance up from down
Not only with sound
But with love, words, music, images and future plans

TREATS OF WINTER

Deep in the forest
We rest on pine-needle blankets
Looking out for spirits, spiders, spell-casters
The coolness, calm atmosphere lain
No winds to mess our hair
Leaning around to gather berries
Rich mauve, maroon and amethyst
Burst the goodness
In your palm, with your fingers
Lapping up the juices
Lips darkening with every fruit
Gulped greedily
Awoken by monsters howling in our frozen faces
Their lair, their food
We are to be ridden
Alas the spirit guide appears in full bloom
Bright, white light interrupts the beasts
On their mission to defeat
The battle begins
The guardian will win
This is our winter

OGRE

Remind me how to be at peace
I ultimately crave the wildebeest
It's not lost in the forest
Or upon my forehead
Be it the principles, a disciple
Nothing more than a twig in the universe
Gaudy and ragged you appear from the moon
I am hoping you don't disappear too soon
I sprint to catch up with him
This stranger from the dark din
And he runs and he runs
And he runs each day
Playing hide and seek
With chins you keep
Your heart in the case
Hiding disgrace
A little more
To taste folklore
Old and wise they lie and lie
I don't know why it is allowed
And they stand proud
Democratic oath and toasts
Judging atheists judging atheists
No care, no clan-blood to poison the dam
Create your own with monster-truck prams
Screeching mouths and wheels on fire
Skull-crushing babies burning their tyres
Mummies and Daddies pushed to delirium
Return each day to peachy oblivion
In fantastic worm-worlds
Checking out girls
All looks and attitudes
Expressing gratitude
Calmly and coolly

Not ugly nor unruly
A permanent place
A wallflower face
To help you continue
Plodding onward to the Core of the Earth
Now and again for her
For her
For them
For you

THE DAY AFTER

Adjust the lights
Shimmering frustration
Too insecure to think or to talk or to smile
So wait awhile

You say "I live to create and give to all
My mind, my heart and wonders small"
But brutality softens the hardened heart and the agony starts
As we watch from a window with a view so HIGH
Tears in my eyes
I begin to cry
My soul has just died

Mama who are you, and why am I telling?
Isn't honesty so compelling?
I have been bruised, and used but then…
So have you
#metoo

THE NEXT DAY AFTER THE DAY AFTER

I'd like to hang off a tropical bed
And let the blood rush to my head
Let it explode into a million pieces
Right into this fear complex

Please give me rosy lenses to see
All the love that's supposed to be for me
The thing that makes this world and me go crazy
Because right now it's so hard to feel it, to feel it is here

It makes insight seem domineering,
And salt from pity tears sting my eyes
I look in the mirror for my own perception
I'll never be able to escape this deposition
They revel and jeer with fiery desperation
But my anger and pride won't let me die
My anger and pride will keep me alive

Today i want to dream, but these pills won't let me
Today i seek redemption, as another bad feeling hits me
Today was only s'posed to be, the same as all the rest
But today turns out to be the day my brain, decided to take the test
Nurse, nurse, when can i rest?
And she says "There are no beds, we'll give you some meds for the end of your journey, as you'll soon be dead!".

SUDDEN DEATH

It will never be the same, since that awful Tuesday
When I woke at midnight
and travelled for milliseconds, seconds, minutes and hours until I found out
what it was like to be a part of something true

the sky seemed darker than usual
driving along familiar roads that looked dreamy and unreal
and this stranger talked to me like I was his old friend
I don't remember his face, the grey hair is all that I can recall
He was more than happy to help me on this journey
I don't know if I have seen him before or after, I guess I'll never know
Because my eyes were too glassy from all the tears and blurry with all the strangeness. It's too much sometimes, to breathe and be alive
What has become of me?
And he says…
"The dusty road to heaven is just a path of doom. And everything that you stand for won't mean anything soon. If you could look into the sky and see what you will be like in the realms of your afterlife. Would you bother still being the same here on earth?"

A happy little chappy with a fun and friendly feeling vibe, he's gone. **VOID**

SELECTING

In the future I will learn to be graceful
Next year will open exciting doors for us
This year has only just started
I see tomorrow features colourful shades of orchard fruits – grape,
    plum, violet, lavender, crimson, pale pale green
And a little bit blue
Core sensations, pass again in
Transience

WHERE WILL THE MOODS TAKE US TOMORROW?

Dreams fulfilled – go to page 95
Obstacles faced – go to page 85
Challenges exciting – go to page 18
Peaceful solitude – go to page 3
Relationship building – go to page 39
Caring and learning – go to page 50

STEFAN

PRISONER

Hurting face
What a disgrace
To all who fought
For their rights in court
Hide away in your shelter
Your pain will only swelter
In a narrow womb
More like a tomb
And you will go on to be
The master of his destiny
But you're always so depressed to me

Just a spec in the universe
Is how you view it
Don't you want to escape this cell
And just do it

Yes bring it to me like I'm really needy
Bless my soul forever
And give me peace
Like you know you want to
Not for any reward
But all because you care

Is this how it starts today?
Can we go back to yesterday
And erase the urge that made us leave?

The shelter of our home was there
And love of kindred spirits fair
But this is where I am now
Please get me out
I shout…

I've never been to the USA
I've never been to the UK
Now they finally acknowledge why
But it's too late because he died

I'm angry that they ignore me
I'm angry that people lie about me
They should mind their own families
Tend to their own abnormalities

Too angry to release a tear
I would rather watch them quickly disappear
You don't like what I've got
Then go rot

Don't be an immature fuck
Trying to drive the wedges
Just eat the wedges instead you fat cunt
Mind your own business
Fuck off and die quickly
So the world can live in reasonable peace
Stop invading my space
Raping the human race
Not having a good day?
My back stands firm, tension in my spine
Watching everyone sideways, glancing in my direction
Just let me be invisible
I do not want your company, your sexuality
Your morals, your substances, your future/past
I only want to follow my regime
Focus my mind on what could be
What could I be?
There are times when I dream about hot potato chips
Or a beer and a cigarette in an ornamental garden…
Looking out in the distance

At the hills, the sea, the trees, even the flies
Then I wake up.
My love appears in dreams
Embracing my brother
My heart aches for commonality, familiarity, comfort
I'm so sick of this darkness
Please give me some light
This mechanical existence is my punishment for trying to provide
For my kin
So I scramble, ramble, struggle on
Shut myself off, till sleep time comes, till Saturday comes
Bless my soul and break this curse
It could be worse
The fear is hopes that won't come true
When the inmates, the officers and the parole board do
What they are programmed to do
And deny me what my family and I crave
No longer be the queen's slave
Then I think of common wealth
And how we are so far away from the original ways
These are new days
Come on and make change
Or return to the old stockade
And leave my body where it lays
With no grave
I thought we had advanced as a nation

With buildings and buses and railway stations
Or are we all just servants of the past?
What are we
Public slaves?
A pool of clotted blood or
an animal caged?
My mind's enraged…
I wonder, I ponder, but…
Lights out.

SAND

Eerie quiet
No wind
Nor people
Just sun
Burning sunshine
Glaring sunlight
Dry heat
Lizard bones
Scales, skin and tails
No tumbleweeds
Nothing
Until
Engine sounds
Getting louder
Dusty, smoky
Wheels roaring out into the
Sunset

MURDERER
baby went hunting
gun in his sling
wearing steel cap boots
a flannel shirt
blue jeans covered in dirt
trekking down the creek bed
tripping on reeds
tracing her footsteps
hungry for flesh
following her scent
no surrender
hands icy
trigger finger cold
shivering
expectations rising
keen concentration
hearing every crinkle
of the woods
flora and fauna
he finds her
he kills her
he buries her in
the end.

ROSES

I was out looking for roses one day
When he went out for sins
We were both just on the edge
But somehow getting in

I was out looking for roses one day
And he went out for daisies
We were both in flower land
So you were already crazy

I was out looking for roses one day
He just went out-a hunting
We drifted away from the flowerbed
And became the weed we never wanted

He went out looking for daisies again
I went back to the edge
Looking for sin and letting everyone in, and
somehow we both survived,
Apart.

LAIR

i am sheltered in the forest
embraced by misty haze and sturdy branches
the greenness is calming
air is still
tranquil, soft and warm
i treasure this, the trees
nature protecting me

STRUGGLE

Heroes walking
Trampling on heroines
Crushed bones
Blood fight lost
Always angered
The hero wins
Gutted fool
Defeated
But not beaten.
Classic

FINAL LINES

I am at one with the universe
Sticking to my guns
Shutting the nuisances out
Competing only with myself
Coping within my mind, body, spirit and heart
Living me
All parts of me
Feeling core sensations
In balance
Ascending to bliss
I see tomorrow
And it looks beautiful

www.ingramcontent.com/pod-product-compliance
Lightning Source LLC
LaVergne TN
LVHW021948060526
838200LV00043B/1960